a HOMEBUILDERS RESOURCE FROM familyLife

LEADER'S GUIDE

PREPARING for marriage

the complete GUIDE to HELP YOU PREPARE
COUPLES FOR a LIFETIME OF LOVE

BY DAVID BOEHI, BRENT NELSON,
Jeff SCHULTE & LLOYD SHADRACH

DENNIS RAINEY

GENERAL EDITOR

Gospel Light

How to Let the Lord Build Your House and not labor in vain.

FamilyLife is a division of Campus Crusade for Christ, Incorporated, an evangelical Christian organization founded in 1951 by Bill Bright. FamilyLife was started in 1976 to help fulfill the Great Commission by strengthening marriages and families and then equipping them to go to the world with the gospel of Jesus Christ. Our FamilyLife Marriage Conference is held in most cities throughout the United States and is one of the fastest-growing marriage conferences in America today. Information on all resources offered by FamilyLife may be obtained by either writing or calling us at the address and telephone number listed below.

GOSPEL LIGHT PUBLISHING STAFF
William T. Greig, Publisher
Dr. Elmer L. Towns, Senior Consulting Publisher
Billie Baptiste, Publisher, Research, Planning and Development
Dr. Gary S. Greig, Wesley Haystead, M.S.Ed.,
   Senior Consulting Editors
Jill Honodel, Editor
Pam Weston, Assistant Editor
Kyle Duncan, Associate Publisher
Bayard Taylor, M.Div., Senior Editor, Theological and Biblical Issues
Debi Thayer, Designer

Preparing for Marriage Leader's Guide
ISBN 0-8307-1760-9
© Copyright 1997 by FamilyLife. All rights reserved.

Dennis Rainey, Executive Director
FamilyLife
P.O. Box 23840
Little Rock, AR 72221-3840
(501) 223-8663

Published by Gospel Light, Ventura, California 93006.
Printed in the U.S.A.

aBOUT tHIS COURSe

Preparing for Marriage was developed by five men working with FamilyLife, a division of Campus Crusade for Christ. FamilyLife's goal is to help you learn practical, biblical blueprints for building a godly home.

The course is part of the HomeBuilders series of small-group studies. The HomeBuilders Couples Series® helps couples learn God's principles for building solid marriages.

Other FamilyLife outreaches include:

"FamilyLife Today" is a 30-minute radio program featuring Dennis Rainey, FamilyLife executive director and the general editor of this study. The show airs five days a week on hundreds of stations across the country.

The FamilyLife Marriage Conferences, weekend getaways for couples, have been attended by hundreds of thousands of people since 1976.

The FamilyLife Parenting Conference helps parents learn how to raise children who will walk with the Lord and develop godly character.

Other practical resources for the family include best-selling books by Dennis Rainey, and Resurrection Eggs®, a popular tool for helping your child learn the true meaning of Easter.

Real FamilyLife magazine provides regular encouragement and help for building a godly home and keeping in touch with FamilyLife's outreaches and resources.

For more information about FamilyLife, call 1-800-FL-TODAY or write us at 3900 N. Rodney Parham, Little Rock, AR 72212. Or you may contact us online at www.familylife-ccc.org.

contents

a message to mentors
from dennis rainey

Consider for a moment the training most teenagers receive to qualify for a driver's license. At the age of 15 (in most states), they can receive a driver's permit if they pass a written test about their state's driving laws. During the next year, they drive under the supervision of a parent or adult. If they are wise, they complete a driver's education course. Through hours of practice, they slowly learn the hundreds of small skills that driving requires: how to accelerate and brake under a variety of conditions, what to observe while driving down the road, how to talk to another person in the car while keeping their eyes on the road, and so much more.

Finally, they must prove their skill by passing a driving test administered by a state licensed inspector. Now they have their prized driver's license in their hands, only to learn that several years of safe driving will be required until they shed the costly mistrust harbored by at least one segment of society—the car insurance companies!

Now consider the requirements for a couple to obtain another type of license. To be legally married, a couple must obtain a blood test and must state their vows of commitment before an ordained minister or a justice of the peace. That's it. If they are wise, they will receive some premarital counseling, but in many churches that means little more than meeting with a pastor to go over the wedding procedures.

What's wrong with this picture?

Our society requires intensive training to receive a driver's license for one simple reason: We know *bad things happen* when we allow someone to drive a car without first learning some critical skills.

Unfortunately, our society is only now waking up to the fact that *bad things happen* when we allow a couple to be married without learning critical relational skills. I could spend pages analyzing all the reasons why America's divorce rate has been the highest of any country in the world for the last 30 years, but it boils down to this: People don't know how to be married. Children are growing up in a culture that emphasizes individuality over responsibility and in families that are increasingly fractured. Because of this they don't learn the skills needed to be able to relate to another person on a daily basis through good times *and* bad, in good health *and* bad, during times of plenty *and* times of need. They have not experienced unconditional love, and our culture and our nation is suffering because of it.

That is why we have developed *Preparing for Marriage* and this accompanying leader's guide. I believe a family reformation can occur in this country as individual families, one home at a time, turn to God's Word as their guide. And the best time to show couples how to allow God to be at the center of their lives and their homes is *before they are married*—before they start to "drive on the streets."

There are few ministries in a church more strategic or effective than guiding couples through the *Preparing for Marriage* workbook and helping them build their homes on the foundation of God's Word.

The Ultimate Marriage Preparation Guide

I'll never forget how a woman who came to me one time for counseling after her divorce described her experience, "You know, as I was preparing for marriage it was as though I started out on this desert landscape. I picked up the binoculars and looked out on the horizon and I could see all of these corpses and all of the rotting flesh and the destruction of broken marriages that had not made it very far across the desert. And even though I could see that so many people hadn't made it very far, I didn't have anyone in my life to grab me by the shoulders and say, 'You need survival training before you start out.' So I started out on the journey with my husband and in a few years found myself in the same condition as these other people who had failed in their relationships."

There are two things I noticed about her comments. First, *she realized that premarriage training would have helped prepare her for the inevitable trials she had faced in her marriage.* Many engaged couples today are apprehensive about this commitment they're about to make. Yes, they may act like they know it all and they may be so consumed with planning a 30-minute ceremony and two-hour reception that you think they wouldn't make the time for premarriage counseling. But they *could* find time with a little encouragement. An increasing number of young people come from broken families themselves, and they want to have successful marriages.

You will find that *Preparing for Marriage* provides the training they need. In fact, it includes the type of material Barbara and I wish we had known before our wedding. By completing *Preparing for Marriage*, couples will:

- Discover the joy of knowing each other and being known at levels they never imagined.
- Learn about how to make a good decision to marry, how to evaluate their relationship and how to discern God's will.
- Talk about things they never dreamed they would discuss but always knew they should.
- Anticipate issues ahead of time instead of being caught off guard after they are married.
- Know, apply and experience God's Word as it relates to engagement and marriage.
- Become confident, certain and secure in their decision to marry (or even not to marry).
- Practice and apply foundational skills they need to build their marriage.
- Acquire some essential communication and conflict resolution skills.
- Understand the critical nature of core roles and responses in marriage.
- Learn about God's design for true sexual intimacy.

The Value of a Mentor

The second thing I learned from this woman was that *she wished someone had been there to give her the type of help she needed.* It was as though she were saying that she needed someone in her life who understood what her needs were and could come alongside with love and compassion—not to preach, but to coach her and help her overcome obstacles in her journey. This person didn't need to be a pastor or counselor; it could have been an older, married friend, or someone from her church—someone willing to take the time to prepare a young woman and young man for a lifetime of marriage.

Whether you are a pastor, a counselor or a lay mentor couple, I am confident you will find this material easy to use as you work with premarried couples. It will guide you systematically through the key issues couples need to learn and discuss before marriage. Plus you will find your involvement personally enriching and rewarding as you sit down with a young couple and prepare them for marriage.

Don't assume you need seminary training to guide a couple through this material. All you need is to be available. I know a large church in Southern California that probably marries about 50 to 60 couples each year. And most of the premarriage training is done by the pastoral staff. This church has not recognized the potential sitting in the pew. With a little training and encouragement, they could use lay couples to meet with these couples. And, frankly, these lay couples may even be able to teach these couples more than the pastors could because many lay couples have more time to devote to these couples. Many pastors lack the time to meet often with a number of couples, but lay couples can often make time to meet with couples many times—both in formal learning sessions and in casual settings—over a period of months.

Preparing to Lead

To guide a couple through *Preparing for Marriage,* you will need to carefully read through the workbook and through this leader's guide. The main sessions and special projects in the workbook are designed so that you have several options for leading them:

- ♥ You can guide the couple personally through the main sessions and have them complete the couple's projects on their own.
- ♥ You can guide a *small group* of couples through the main sessions and have them complete the couple's projects on their own.
- ♥ You can have a couple complete the main sessions on their own and then meet with you for discussion.

However you use this material, we are confident that you will find premarriage training a great adventure. You don't need years of training nor do you need a special degree. All you need is the willingness to be available—to teach, to train, to model, to encourage and to love. You can do it, with Christ's help!

Overview of Preparing for Marriage

goals

As we created *Preparing for Marriage*, our first goal was to provide a quality, entertaining and thorough premarital curriculum that furnishes premarried couples with the important information and training they need before marriage. Part of the material for this study was taken from the FamilyLife Marriage Conference, but then we also conducted interviews with premarried couples, pastors and premarital counselors and examined numerous premarried curriculums from churches across the country.

We've found that many couples get married with only a scant understanding of God's blueprints for the home. That's why Sessions One and Two in the workbook focus on God's purposes and plan for marriage. In addition, the curriculum includes interactive questions designed to help couples develop their communication skills. The "Couple's Projects" at the end of each session give couples the opportunity to discuss what they are learning and determine how it applies to their relationship. Five "Special Projects" are included to guide couples in digging deeper into such topics as understanding the past, uncovering their expectations and discerning God's will for their relationship.

The workbook includes six regular sessions and five special projects. This in itself is a statement of the importance of marriage preparation. While most couples who do receive premarital counseling today only meet one or two times with a counselor, an increasing number of churches are recognizing the need for more extensive training. A survey by *Marriage Partnership* magazine of 3,000 couples from 25 denominations who had received premarital counseling, revealed the importance of extensive premarital counseling. One question asked "Did your premarital counseling help you in marriage?" The following is a breakdown of those who answered "definitely yes":

One counseling session received	15%
Two sessions received	31%
Five sessions received	53%
Seven or more sessions received	75%

Our second goal is to provide couples with the opportunity to learn from a mentor or mentoring couple. Couples begin with a vow to make their marriages succeed, but many unknowingly repeat many of the same errors their parents made, ending up with a marriage far from what they had envisioned.

Premarried couples face a great uphill battle. Cultural, economic and career pressures intensify the struggles they face in adjusting to each other. In most cases they will not discuss or even recognize these difficulties until the eleventh hour.

We are convinced that if churches want to help couples build strong marriages and families, they need to connect those couples with godly, older mentors who have already been down the same path. You don't need to be a pastor or a trained counselor to lead a couple through this workbook. If you are walking with God and if your marriage is on solid ground, you can do it.

As a mentor for premarried couples, you can help counter the years of poor training many individuals have had. By allowing couples access to your lives and your marriage, allowing them to ask questions, you can show these couples how a marriage between two imperfect people can work. They can observe firsthand what commitment to a godly, satisfying marriage relationship looks like.

The material in this course is formatted so that you become a facilitator, not a teacher. You don't need a seminary degree or counseling experience. All you need is a desire to help guide couples through the material, and then make yourself available as a resource and friend. Your involvement in their lives may have a greater impact than anything else they learn in this course.

Our final goal is to challenge couples to seriously and honestly evaluate whether God really is calling them to marriage. Let's be honest. It's very difficult for most couples to keep their heads clear during courtship and engagement. Many couples are so swept up in the emotions that they fail to take time to honestly evaluate their relationship and decide whether God is calling them together. In fact, many couples lack a clear understanding of how to determine God's will.

As you will see, this course requires a good deal of homework involving both personal study and couple interaction. This material raises important questions and helps couples address difficult issues. We've found that couples enjoy the time together and are grateful to discuss important topics they had not previously discussed together.

We've also included a "Decision-Making Guide" that provides clear, step-by-step directions to help couples evaluate their relationship and seek the will of God.

When they complete the course, many couples will discover that God has used the material to reveal His will and confirm their decision. Some, however, will find that they should postpone or cancel their wedding. Such decisions are difficult, but they protect these couples from a great deal of heartache down the road.

format

Preparing for Marriage includes two primary components:

Main Sessions

In each of the six main sessions couples will learn more about how to make a marriage work and then interact with each other to apply the material to their relationship. These sessions are contained in parts two and three of the workbook.

Here's what you will find in each session:

> **True North**—A statement of the biblical truth related to the topic you are covering
>
> **Get the Picture**—An introduction to the topic that gives them the opportunity to answer questions and complete exercises that allow them to grasp the topic and understand why it is important
>
> **Get the Truth**—The Bible discovery section of each chapter in which they examine and discuss biblical truths to learn God's principles on different aspects of marriage
>
> **Navigating by True North: Truths to Chart Your Course**—Summary statements of the key principles from each session
>
> **Couple's Project**—The interaction portion of the session that includes the following sections:
>
> > **Get Real**: Questions to guide discussion.
> >
> > **Get to the Heart of Your Marriage—Prayer**: An opportunity to pray together and experience a spiritual discipline that will be one of the keys to their growing marriage in the years to come.
> >
> > **Get Deeper**: Optional assignments for the highly motivated—those who want to go where no engaged couple has gone before!
> >
> > **Questions for Those Who Were Previously Married**

In addition, several of the sessions include bonus projects designed to help couples deepen their experience as they work through the course.

Special Projects

These five projects will guide couples in discussions of critical issues and help them learn even more about one another. These projects include:

- The "Personal History Worksheet" has dozens of questions designed to help them understand their past and share it with one another.
- The "Great Expectations" helps a couple understand the expectations they are bringing into their marriage.
- "Evaluating Your Relationship" provides a framework to ask some challenging questions about their relationship.

- "A Decision-Making Guide" is designed to help them discern God's will for their relationship.
- The "Purity Covenant" provides an opportunity to commit themselves to sexual purity before they are married.

Two other notes regarding format: First, in order to receive the most benefit from this course, we strongly recommend that each person obtain a personal workbook. Second, the word, "fiancé(e)" has been chosen to represent both the man or woman as in "Meet with your fiancé(e) to discuss your answers." We realize this word may feel a bit strange, but we figure you'll be able to overlook that awkwardness as you work through this study.

LenGth of the course

While the course can be completed in six weeks, we recommend completing one session every two weeks, so the course will last about 12 weeks.

This time frame requires a high level of commitment from both the church and the premarried couple. The church will need to offer the course well in advance of a couple's wedding date; we recommend completing it at least one month before that date, if not longer. Couples, meanwhile, will need to plan an engagement long enough to incorporate at least 12 weeks of training, plus at least one month after the sessions end. We realize they may not be happy about completing such a long course, but if you do a good job of selling the advantages of this approach they should embrace it.

three options for using the workbook

While a couple can complete the workbook on their own, the guidance of a pastor, counselor or mentor will make the experience much more rewarding.

However you use the workbook, we recommend that you begin by meeting with the couple for "The Opening Interview" (see pages 37-56). Then there are three options for you to consider as you prepare the course.

Option A with One Couple

You guide the couple through the main content of each session—
"Get the Picture" and "Get the Truth"—then have them complete
the Couple's Projects on their own.

SUGGESTED SEQUENCE

First Meeting:	Opening Interview
	Assign Special Project 1
Second Meeting:	Work through Session One with the couple
	Discuss Special Project 1: Personal History Worksheet
Third Meeting:	Work through Session Two with the couple
	Assign Special Project 2
Fourth Meeting:	Work through Session Three with the couple
	Discuss Special Project 2: Great Expectations
	Assign Special Project 3
Fifth Meeting:	Work through Session Four with the couple
	Discuss Special Project 3: Evaluating Your Relationship
	Assign Special Project 4
Sixth Meeting:	Work through Session Five with the couple
	Discuss Special Project 4: A Decision-Making Guide
Seventh Meeting:	Work through Session Six with the couple
	Discuss any final questions

Option B with One Couple

Each person completes the main content—"Get the Picture" and
"Get the Truth"— of each session individually, then the couple works
together to complete the Couple's Project. Finally, the couple meets
with you to discuss what they learned. You will find suggestions for

how to lead this discussion in section two of this mentor's guide.

The suggested sequence for this option is very similar to Option A:

First Meeting:	Opening Interview
	Assign Session One and
	Special Project 1
Second Meeting:	Discuss Session One
	Discuss Special Project 1:
	Personal History Worksheet
	Assign Session Two
Third Meeting:	Discuss Session Two
	Assign Session Three and
	Special Project 2
Fourth Meeting:	Discuss Session Three
	Discuss Special Project 2:
	Great Expectations
	Assign Session Four and
	Special Project 3
Fifth Meetinge:	Discuss Session Four
	Discuss Special Project 3:
	Evaluating Your Relationship
	Assign Session Five and
	Special Project 4
Sixth Meeting:	Discuss Session Five
	Discuss Special Project 4:
	A Decision-Making Guide
	Assign Session Six and Final Project
Seventh Meeting:	Discuss Session Six
	Discuss any final questions

Option C with Small Group

You lead a small group of couples through "Get the Picture" and "Get the Truth" in each session. Each couple meets on their own to complete the Couple's Project. Then you meet with each couple individually at least four more times between the group sessions to ask them more personal questions about how they've applied the material in their relationship. You will find suggestions for conducting the personal meetings in section two of this counselor's guide.

SUGGESTED SEQUENCE

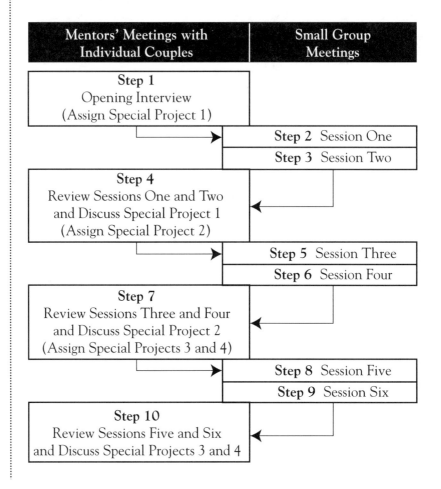

Mentors' Meetings with Individual Couples	Small Group Meetings
Step 1 Opening Interview (Assign Special Project 1)	
	Step 2 Session One
	Step 3 Session Two
Step 4 Review Sessions One and Two and Discuss Special Project 1 (Assign Special Project 2)	
	Step 5 Session Three
	Step 6 Session Four
Step 7 Review Sessions Three and Four and Discuss Special Project 2 (Assign Special Projects 3 and 4)	
	Step 8 Session Five
	Step 9 Session Six
Step 10 Review Sessions Five and Six and Discuss Special Projects 3 and 4	

a note about couples who have been married previously

When someone has been married before, he or she brings a new set of issues into a new marriage, especially if the first marriage ended in divorce. Most of the material in this study applies to previously married couples as much as it does to couples who have not been married before. The bigger challenge, however, is getting them to discuss the more difficult topics such as analyzing the mistakes of the first marriage and, if applicable, coming to grips with the realities of a blended family.

Many of these issues will come to light through the special questions for previously married couples in the Couple's Projects at the end of each session. You will want to look through the sessions and look for ways to adapt the material to the couple you are mentoring.

There are two key issues that couples who have been divorced need to face. First, *they need to admit their own responsibility in the failure of their previous marriage.* Many people want to put the blame on the ex-spouse so they are unwilling to see their own part in the failure of the previous marriage.

Second, *they need to recognize the errors they made in the previous marriage so they can trust God to change them and make it possible to build a better marriage this time around.* Otherwise they will repeat the same patterns that led to divorce in the first marriage.

One special note: Some of the questions are geared toward those who are divorced. If this is not the situation with the couple you are mentoring, that is if one or both of them are widowed, lead them to those questions that *will* apply to their situation.

tips for Leading a small group

1. Each session is designed for a time block of approximately 90 minutes. This would allow you 75 minutes for small-group discussion and 15 minutes for refreshments and fellowship. If you want to allow couples to work on their Couple's Projects immediately after the small-group time, add another 30 minutes to your schedule.

   Once the couples in your group get to know each other and interaction gets underway, you may find it more difficult to complete a session in the time allotted. You'll need to determine ahead of time which questions are most important for you to cover.

2. If you're using this material in a Sunday School time period of approximately 60 minutes, you can adapt the time by taking two weeks to complete each session.

3. Remember that you are not a teacher in this study; you are a *facilitator*. While you'll be sharing from your own knowledge and experience quite often, your goal is to encourage couples to learn the material themselves as they look up Bible passages and discuss the different concepts. You will need to learn the material thoroughly, however, so that you can keep the discussion on the right track and ensure that the couples are understanding the principles and concepts.

4. Do not let the sessions drag, become dull and boring, or go too long. Be sensitive to the needs of the group and watch their attention span—when people stop contributing, they may have stopped listening as well. It is far better for people to wish the session could have gone longer than for them to wish it had ended sooner. Keep it moving. Keep it lively. Keep it going!

5. Don't be afraid of a question that is greeted with group silence—some of the best answers come after a few moments of silent thought. Keep in mind as a group leader that 15 seconds can seem like five minutes when you are waiting for an answer to a thought-provoking question.

6. If you find one or two particularly profound questions that you really want everyone to think about, have group members pause to consider the question individually and then write and share their answers with the group. Moments of silence and self-evaluation can be among the sharpest tools for truly teaching others, but use these moments strategically *and* sparingly.

7. Be sensitive to your use of time and be careful not to make comments about time pressure that will make the group feel rushed. When you need to move the discussion to the next item, say something like: "We could probably talk about that question the rest of the evening, but we need to consider several other important questions."

    When it is necessary to reduce or eliminate the time spent on a later question, simply say, "You can see that there are several more questions we could have moved on to discuss, but I felt we were making real progress, so I chose to spend some extra time on the earlier points."

You are the leader of your group and know the needs of the individual couples best. But keep in mind that the Holy Spirit will have an agenda for couples that you may never know about. "The mind of man plans his way, but the LORD directs his steps" (Proverbs 16:9). Do your best to prepare and pray over the session and then leave the results to God.

8. You'll find many open-ended discussions throughout the study. One way to help stimulate discussion is to prepare some answers to these questions yourself. If you ask a question and nobody answers at first, give your own perspective and then open the discussion up to others.

C h a p t e r   T w o

mINIStERING to PREmaRRIED CouPLes

Do you remember your own courtship and engagement? For many of us, it was an experience like no other—a time of great excitement, joy, romance and anticipation, but it was also a time of intense pressure and raw nerves.

As you look back upon this time now, however, you may be able to see it through different eyes. Were you caught up in the usual whirlwind of activities leading up to the wedding? Were you well prepared for the marriage you were about to begin? Did you really know each other very well? Would you do anything differently now?

There are many engaged couples who are well prepared for marriage, but as you guide couples through the workbook, you would be wise to assume that they don't realize what they don't know. They need your guidance to prepare them for the most important of human relationships in their lives on earth.

THINGS TO REMEMBER ABOUT PREMARRIEDS

1. Many engaged couples are *wearing blinders*. An engaged person is often aware of negative characteristics in the one he or she loves, but figures, "It won't be like that when we're married."

2. Many engaged couples approach marriage with an *idealistic* view of how perfect their marriage will be, but they are not aware of the potential problems, arguments, disagreements, and so on that occur as two become one.

3. Because of the hectic schedule leading up to the wedding and honeymoon, engaged couples are experiencing one of the most *stressful* times of their lives.

4. Many engaged couples are staying up later than normal during the time before the wedding and therefore are getting *little sleep*. This, naturally, puts extra pressure on their relationship and on their interactions with others.

5. Many couples, whether they realize it or not, have demonstrated a *willingness to sacrifice some biblical values for the sake of the relationship*. A large number of engaged couples, for example, are already having sexual intercourse when they begin premarital counseling.

6. Those who are not already having intercourse are struggling with keeping their desires in check. They are *physically charged, yet fatigued*, making it even more difficult for them to draw boundaries and know when to stop.

7. Before most couples reach the altar, they usually endure *a time of financial pressure as a result of wedding expenses*. Everything seems to cost more than it should, or that's often what at least one partner thinks.

8. Even though engaged couples have discussed many things during their courtship and engagement, *many have talked very little about normal financial habits and expenses*. As a result, they will often be surprised by the habits of their new spouse once they are married.

9. Most couples struggle with *extremes in emotions*. For some women these emotions are amplified by reactions to birth control pills.

10. Many are so caught up in their excitement that they *fail to think rationally* about their future mates. They pass over potential problems that could sabotage the relationship, believing instead that "love conquers all."

11. They are *not acutely aware of their idealistic expectations* about the relationship and the marriage. As a result, they're setting themselves up for disappointment when reality sets in.

12. A significant number of *couples have discussed only in part how their past has affected them.* Many don't know about serious relational baggage they are bringing into the marriage.

13. *Those who begin to have doubts about whether this marriage is right will feel tremendous pressure to go ahead with the wedding anyway.* Some of this pressure will come from family members who have already made plans and spent money on the wedding. Then again much of the pressure is self-induced because they don't want to cause problems for their friends and family, or they don't want to be embarrassed by publicly admitting a failure. Women in their mid to late 30s may feel this is their "last chance" to find a mate and begin a family.

And finally...

14. *Many couples are* not *excited about premarital counseling.* They consider it a necessary evil, just another thing they need to squeeze in to an already busy schedule. They also think they already know it all anyway!

goals in ministering to premarried couples

GOAL ONE: WORK TO REPLACE THE IDEALIZED VIEW OF MARRIAGE WITH A MORE REALISTIC VIEW.

In his book *Communication: Key to Your Marriage*, H. Norman Wright says:

> Too many young couples enter marriage blinded by unrealistic expectations. They believe the relationship should be characterized by a high level of continuous romantic love. As one young adult said: "I wanted marriage to

fulfill all my desires. I needed security, someone to take care of me, intellectual stimulation, economic security immediately—but it just wasn't like that!" People are looking for something "magical" to happen in marriage. But magic doesn't make a marriage work: hard work does.[1]

You don't want to destroy their idealism, but you do need to help them honestly evaluate their relationship. They need to see that the result of a lifelong commitment is that they will go through a lot of trials, problems and heartaches as well as joy, fun and excitement.

GOAL TWO: HELP THE COUPLE COME TO AN HONEST DECISION ABOUT WHETHER GOD IS REALLY CALLING THEM TOGETHER.

During the course of this study, couples may learn more about each other than they had ever dreamed possible. And yet even then they'll be barely scratching the surface! Your job will be to guide them through the process and encourage them to be open to God's leading. Encourage them to take their time, and not feel pressured to get engaged or married.

One key ingredient to this study that you may find surprising is that *it is designed to bring difficult questions, doubts or qualms to the surface.* We want to ask questions that leave couples uneasy, forcing them to honestly face whether this is God's will for them. Too many couples fail to ask the tough questions this study will raise, and they pay the price for this failure.

GOAL THREE: GIVE THEM A GLIMPSE OF YOUR OWN MARRIAGE RELATIONSHIP.

This is especially important if anyone you work with comes from a broken home. This individual may never have seen a marriage work the way it should; your relationship may be the first biblically based model he or she has observed. As you work with an engaged couple, spend time with them apart from your scheduled meetings. Invite them over for dinner or go out with them on a double date. Let them see how you relate to one another and to your children.

Give them the freedom to ask you tough questions. Share your mistakes as well as your triumphs. Tell them how you've resolved conflict, how you've made decisions together and how you've faced various types of trials.

GOAL FOUR: HOLD THEM ACCOUNTABLE.

Accountability is a scriptural principle that tells us to "be subject to one another in the fear of Christ" (Ephesians 5:21). This means I choose to submit my life to the scrutiny of another person to gain spiritual strength, growth and balance.

Accountability means asking the other person for advice. It means giving the other person the freedom to make honest observations and evaluations about you. It means we're teachable and approachable.

Accountability is a key ingredient of this course, and you must establish it at the very beginning. You can do this in two ways: First, let them know what is expected of them, and secondly, follow through each time you meet to see if they've completed their assignments.

Let them know from the beginning that they are free to ask you about anything, and that you will take the freedom to ask *them* about anything. As you work with the couple, different issues will undoubtedly surface. It's important for you to hold them accountable to discussing and resolving these issues as much as possible. For example, if you discover that one person wants to have a large family but the other is hesitant to even have children, you need to hold them accountable to work through that issue *before* they are married. Follow up by asking them if they've discussed it and what decisions they've made.

Emphasize the importance of completing the homework assigned each session. If you see the couple consistently coming to the sessions with incomplete homework, note it as a danger signal and set up an additional session with them to discuss any potential problems. Also, you'll need to determine ahead of time how many sessions you will allow a couple to miss and how they can make up sessions they miss.

Accountability will also help couples maintain sexual purity before marriage. Don't be afraid to ask them if they've been able to keep their hands off each other!

suggested tools
and resources

Personality/Temperament Tests

Taylor-Johnson Temperament Analysis
Robert M. Taylor and Lucile Philips Morrison
Psychological Publications, Inc.
5300 Hollywood Blvd.
Los Angeles, CA 90027

PREPARE Test
PREPARE Inc.,
P. O. Box 190
Minneapolis, MN 55440

Myers-Briggs Type Indicator®
Consulting Psychologists Press
3803 East Bayshore Road
Palo Alto, CA 94303
800-624-1765

Recommended Books on Marriage and Premarriage

It is recommended that some of the following books and Bible study materials be added to your church library to be available for both mentors and couples. Books indicated with an * are suggested readings for the workbook Couple's Projects "Get Deeper" sections. Having these five books on hand for couples to borrow would encourage them to delve into the "Get Deeper" activities.

Neil T. Anderson and Charles Mylander, *The Christ-Centered Marriage*, Regal Books, 1996

Ron Blue, *Master Your Money*, Thomas Nelson Inc., 1993

Larry Burkett, *The Financial Planning Workbook*, Moody Press, 1990

*Larry Burkett with Michael E. Taylor, *Money Before Marriage*, Moody Press, 1991

Gary Chapman, *The Five Love Languages*, Northfield Publishing, 1995

*Robert Lewis and William Hendricks, *Rocking the Roles*, NavPress, 1991

*Dennis Rainey with David Boehi, *The Tribute and The Promise*, Thomas Nelson Inc., 1994

*Dennis Rainey, *Staying Close*, Word Publishing, 1989

Dennis and Barbara Rainey, *Building Your Mate's Self-Esteem*, Thomas Nelson Inc., 1993

Dennis and Barbara Rainey, *Moments Together for Couples*, Regal Books, 1995

Wes Roberts and H. Norman Wright, *Before You Say I Do*, Harvest House Publishers, 1997

*Ed and Gaye Wheat, *Intended for Pleasure*, Fleming H. Revell Co., 1981

H. Norman Wright, *Communication: Key to Your Marriage*, Regal Books, 1974

H. Norman Wright, *So You're Getting Married*, Regal Books, 1985

H. Norman Wright, *Starting Out Together: A Devotional for Dating and Engaged Couples*, Regal Books, 1996

Recommended Bible Study Curriculum for Before and After Marriage

THE HOMEBUILDERS COUPLES SERIES®
For small group Bible studies from Gospel Light Publications

Building Teamwork in Your Marriage
> by Robert Lewis

Building Your Marriage
> by Dennis Rainey

Building Your Mate's Self-Esteem
> by Dennis and Barbara Rainey

Expressing Love in Your Marriage
> by Jerry and Sheryl Wunder and Dennis and
>
> Jill Eenigenburg

Growing Together in Christ
> by David Sunde

Life Choices for a Lasting Marriage
> by David Boehi

Managing Pressure in Your Marriage
> by Dennis Rainey and Robert Lewis

Mastering Money in Your Marriage
> by Ron Blue

Resolving Conflict in Your Marriage
> by Bob and Jan Horner

HOMEBUILDERS COUPLES SERIES® BIBLE STUDY ELECTIVES

For Sunday School classes or Bible study groups from Gospel Light Publications

Building Teamwork in Your Marriage
> by Robert Lewis

Building Your Marriage
> by Dennis Rainey

Building Your Mate's Self-Esteem (with optional video)
> by Dennis and Barbara Rainey

Growing Together in Christ
> by David Sunde

ADDITIONAL STUDIES

Available from Gospel Light Publications

Neil T. Anderson and Chuck Mylander, *The Christ-Centered Marriage Study Guide*

H. Norman Wright, *Communication: Key to Your Marriage* and *More Communication Keys for Your Marriage Group Study Guide*

H. Norman Wright, *The Marriage Renewal Video Series*

Conferences

We recommend all couples try to attend a FamilyLife Marriage Conference in the city nearest them and closest to their anticipated wedding date in order to be fully equipped with God's blueprints for marriage. For more information call 1-800-FL-TODAY.

1. H. Norman Wright, *Communication: Key to Your Marriage* (Ventura, Calif., Regal Books, 1974), Introduction.

USING
mentors

In most churches, pastors handle all the premarried counseling. But one of the most significant trends of the church today is equipping laypeople to be involved in mentoring.

Recently FamilyLife hired a professional to help us form focus groups to learn how we could better strengthen families. The results of the research were startling. We asked couples what they felt they needed to make their marriages and families successful. One by one they all said pretty much the same thing: They wanted a mentor—someone who had already been through their phase of life and could guide them.

They wanted a real, live person of whom they could ask questions—about resolving conflicts, about babies sleeping through the night, about romance and sex after you start having families, about balancing the demands of work and family, about solving sibling rivalry.

The same goes for premarried couples. Many have no idea how to make a marriage work because they've never seen one modeled.

Many come from broken or dysfunctional homes, and they are afraid that they will repeat the same pattern.

In the midst of the crisis that swirls around family issues, the Church is sitting on an untapped gold mine of couples who have been married five or more years. These couples—especially those who have been married more than 15 years—need to be challenged to pour their lives into younger couples, both married and premarried. But many lack confidence or feel they have nothing to offer. They need a passionate challenge and a little training to be ready to provide counseling to young couples.

Mentoring couples can take a load off the pastor and make the premarital counseling ministry one of the most dynamic in the church. Many churches who have been using the field test version of this workbook have become sold on the concept of mentoring.

Yes, there will be some situations that mentoring couples will not be equipped to handle. But we've found that the large majority of premarried couples benefit tremendously from exposure to a mentoring couple who guides them through the study and into a biblically centered marriage.

fINDINg mENTORINg coupLes

Look around your church. Who comes to mind when you think of healthy Christian marriages? Are there any people who have a desire to help reach other families? Who has the ability to relate to younger couples and remember what it was like to be in their shoes, before and after marriage? Who has experience in leading small groups?

Here are some specifics of what to look for:

- People with the spiritual gifts of exhortation, encouragement, discernment, teaching or shepherding;
- Couples with a desire to help others learn what has worked for them;
- People with a passion for the Lord and an ability to live out biblical principles in their lives and their marriages;
- Couples married five years or more, especially couples in your church whose children are grown and who have the desire and ability to minister to younger couples;

- Couples who demonstrate that their own marriages are growing relationships;
- Couples who are willing to acknowledge their own struggles as well as their successes;
- People with good interpersonal skills and initiative who have a willingness and the time to build friendships with these young couples by meeting with them outside the main sessions;
- People with a willingness to lovingly confront and discuss difficult issues pertaining to marriage;
- People who have participated or led previous small groups and can recognize the difference between *teaching* material and *leading a group discussion* about that material;
- People who are teachable and willing to allow God to work through them to touch the lives of young couples.

After you have recruited some mentor couples and prior to beginning the course, meet with them and discuss the following:

- The importance of their role;
- Where they might need further training;
- The difference between a "lecture approach" and a "facilitator approach;" (Couples who have gone through premarital counseling have asked that the content be interactive. They need time to talk it out with the leaders, each other and other couples facing the same new adventure of marriage. So the role of the mentoring couples during the small group interaction is one of discussion leader rather than teacher.)
- The subject matter—using the rough outlines for the sessions and projects;
- How the personality testing will be handled;
- Who will conduct the opening interview;
- Up-to-date information on church wedding policies;
- When and how needed training and information about working with premarried couples will be available;
- What preparation they will need in handling delicate issues such as divorce, sexual intimacy, whether this

marriage is right, etc. Discuss when they need to talk to you about problems that might surface;

• Any books or articles that you would recommend to them in preparing for their role.

Do not overwhelm the mentoring couples. Sort out and prepare what you think is the most important preparation for them.

As a leader you will serve these mentors well if you monitor their progress by doing the following:

• Sit in on one of their sessions if you can.
• Give them positive and constructive feedback.
• Talk with them regularly.
• Encourage them further in their own marriages.

tHe OpeNINg INterview

geNeraL comments

1. The opening interview is divided into two sections: "Personal Questions" and "Course Overview." You should complete this interview with the couple before they begin the sessions in the workbook. *Do not give a copy of the interview to the couple; it is designed for you to ask the questions verbally and make note of their answers.* You have permission to photocopy the interview pages for each time you do an opening interview.

2. As previously stated, there are four goals to this interview:

    ♥ To give you the opportunity to begin developing a relationship with the couple;
    ♥ To learn more about the couple and how they have reached this point in their relationship;
    ♥ To let the couple know about the course and its requirements;
    ♥ To determine whether the couple is ready to begin the course.

The fourth goal is, of course, a difficult one to quantify. While conducting the interview, you may begin to develop some serious doubts about whether this couple is making a wise decision. Don't break in immediately and begin counseling or exhorting. Continue the questions and let the couple continue to talk and build trust in you. Then, take advantage of the changes of subject during the Personal Questions to sensitively inject some personal questions or comments.

3. We suggest setting aside at least two hours for this interview to allow enough time for the couple to answer the questions and for you to develop a relationship. You could include lunch or dinner in the first part of your meeting, but do not ask the questions in the section on Moral Guidelines while in a public place.

4. After you have explained the course format, be sure to encourage the couple to complete the first two Special Projects—"Evaluating Your Relationship" and "Personal History Worksheet"—before they begin the main sessions.

5. Begin the interview by telling them a little about yourself, your marriage and your family. Commend them for taking the time to evaluate their potential marriage, then begin the Personal Questions section.

Personal Questions

1. The questions in "History of the Relationship" give you the opportunity to evaluate the depth and strength of the couple's relationship. As they describe how they met and how their relationship developed, your job is to listen and draw them out. Jot down notes about the strengths and weaknesses you perceive in the relationship. Also listen for comments that may indicate potential problems and be sure to address these areas in the future.

2. "Spiritual History" will help you evaluate each partner's spiritual beliefs and convictions. Be sure to encourage both of them to talk so you can see if one person seems much more mature in this area than the other.

    If, after completing question 3, you are concerned that one or both partners may not be Christians, this would be a good opportunity for you to explain the plan of salvation. If they appear to be young or immature in their faith, talk to them after completing question 5. In either case, recommend that the couple complete a study on the fundamentals of the Christian faith with you or with someone in the church. Also, ask them to wait at least six months before pursuing any wedding plans. Explain the benefits to them: As they learn more about how to build a relationship with God, the foundation of their potential union will only become stronger.

3. The section on "Moral Guidelines" is a sensitive area because many premarried couples are either sleeping together already or if they are not, they have very loose boundaries about their behavior. This is the first of at least three opportunities to challenge couples in this area—you will also revisit the subject briefly in Session Two and more thoroughly in Session Six.

   Important Note: Be sure to avoid asking these questions in a public place, where a couple will probably feel reluctant to discuss personal matters.

   In most cases, we encourage you to take this opportunity to challenge the couple strongly in this area because we feel that sexual involvement before marriage not only violates God's commandments but also prevents them from making a clear decision about how He is leading in their relationship.

   Watch each person closely as you discuss the following issue and especially as you ask about their physical involvement. You may catch some people off guard when you ask them this question and their reaction may be revealing. Others may anticipate the fact that you will ask them about sex and may not answer truthfully. Do not hesitate to ask about specifics as they respond.

   Unless you sense that it would not be wise at this time, encourage the couple to complete "Special Project 5: The Purity Covenant" located in the appendix of the personal workbook. In this project they look closely at God's desire for them to be sexually pure before marriage and they sign a commitment to do so until their honeymoon. Either have the couple sign this commitment in your presence or tell them you'll be asking them about it during your next meeting.

   If you decide not to challenge them to complete the Purity Covenant at this time, use your judgment on when to talk to them about it. You might want to wait until the end of Session Two when the subject comes up again. We do not, however, recommend waiting until the end of the study. This is an issue that needs to be confronted quickly.

Course Overview

1. In this section, you tell them about the course. Begin by reading to them the material about the goals and significance of the course on page 11 (see also page 51). Explain the concept of mentoring to them.

    If one or both of them have been married previously, tell them that most of the principles in the workbook will apply to them just as they would to any other premarried couple. They do, however, have additional questions located at the end of each Couple's Project that will help them discuss some key areas directly related to their relationship.

2. When you reach the section on format, begin by showing them a copy of the workbook. If you know the couple will be going through the study with you, go ahead and give them their copies at this time. Show them how the workbook is put together and explain each part—the six sessions and the special projects. Then talk to them about how the course will work, according to how you are using it (see options on pages 15-18). If possible, set up the next date when you will meet.

3. Explain that the course requires a high degree of effort and accountability. They should, however, enjoy the experience as much as they will benefit from it.

    Ask the couple if they feel they can make the commitment to this study. If they hesitate because of a busy schedule, find out what commitments they are facing currently. Talk through these and challenge them to set aside some other commitments in order to make this study a priority.

4. If you have a church policy on setting a wedding date, let them know it. If you do not currently have a policy, here's our recommendation: State that because marriage is such a serious proposition, you need to reserve the right to recommend that they postpone a wedding if necessary. Tell them that they are free to set a date, but they should set it far enough in advance that they could easily postpone the wedding if issues

arise during the course that lead you to conclude that they need more time before they marry.

A common "point of no return" in the minds of many couples is the date when wedding invitations are mailed. If a couple sets a date for at least two months after the end of the course, that would allow them enough time to postpone the date if necessary before sending out the invitations.

5.   Give the couple a brochure for the FamilyLife Marriage Conferences and urge them to attend one if possible. You can obtain current brochures from FamilyLife by calling 1-800-FL-TODAY.

Additional Tips

1.   If your mate will be involved with you in this mentoring relationship, conduct the initial interview together.

2.   Many premarried couples will be nervous about this initial meeting. Look for ways to get them to be relaxed and honest with their answers.

3.   Adjust your comments depending on whether the couple is engaged or not.

4.   Explain your role, letting the couple know that you have their best interests and the success of their future marriage at heart. You want them to enjoy success in their marriage and that is why from time to time you will be evaluating their responses to one another and possibly sharing some difficult information with them.

OPENING INTERVIEW

Interviewer _____

Date _____

Personal Information

Name _____Age _____

Address _____

City _____ State _____ Zip _____

Phone (home)_____(office) _____

Vocation _____

Name _____Age _____

Address _____

Phone (home)_____(office) _____

Vocation _____

Are they engaged?   ❑ Yes   ❑ No

If so, what is their anticipated wedding date? _____

personaL questions

History of the Relationship

1.   How did you meet? How long have you been dating each other?

2.   What kinds of dates have you had? (types of activities; whether they primarily spent time alone or with other people, etc.)

3.   Briefly tell about your families.

Are your parents still alive?

Do you have brothers or sisters? How many?

Are any of your brothers or sisters already married?

4. How would you evaluate your parents' marriage?

_____

_____

_____

_____

5. How well have you gotten to know each other's families?

_____

_____

_____

_____

6. How do your family and friends feel about your relationship?

_____

_____

_____

_____

7. Have you ever broken off your relationship?

_____

Why did this happen?

_____

Why did you get back together?

_____

8. Why did you decide to marry each other?
   (OR: Why are you considering marrige?)

_____

_____

_____

_____

9. Why do you think this marriage will work?

    _____

    _____

    _____

    _____

10. What preparation for marriage have you had?

    _____

    _____

    _____

    _____

11. What do you hope to receive from this premarriage preparation course?

    _____

    _____

    _____

    _____

12. What concerns or problems do you feel need to be worked through in your relationship?

    _____

    _____

    _____

    _____

13. Is there anything that you would like to ask or share that we haven't discussed?

    _____

    _____

    _____

    _____

14. Have you been married before?
    If so, were you widowed or divorced?

    _____

    _____

    _____

    _____

    If you were divorced…

    ♥ How did it end?

    _____

    _____

    _____

    ♥ When was your divorce finalized?

    _____

    _____

    _____

    _____

    ♥ Has your previous partner remarried?

    _____

    _____

    _____

    _____

    ♥ Can you identify any failings that contributed to the break-
      down of your previous marriage?

    _____

    _____

    _____

    _____

♥ What have you done to resolve those issues?

_____

_____

_____

_____

♥ Do you have any children from this previous marriage?

_____

_____

_____

_____

♥ What living arrangement has been determined for the children?

_____

Is that a good working relationship for all parties concerned? Why or why not?

_____

_____

_____

_____

Spiritual Background

1. Tell me about your church and spiritual background.

_____

_____

_____

_____

2. This church is committed to building strong marriages with Christ at the center. Why do you think Jesus Christ came to earth?

_____

_____

_____

_____

3. What effect has Jesus Christ had on your life?

_____

_____

_____

_____

What is your relationship with Jesus Christ right now?

_____

_____

_____

_____

Is He your personal Savior and Lord?

_____

_____

_____

_____

4. What part has Jesus Christ played in your dating relationship?

_____

_____

_____

_____

5.   What part do you expect Christ to play in your marriage?

_____

_____

_____

_____

Moral Guidelines

> **Note: Be sure to NOT discuss the following questions in a public place.**

1.   As couples grow closer to each other emotionally and spiritually, the natural response is to move closer to each other physically. God intends this area of our lives to be enjoyed to the fullest, but within the context of marriage (see Hebrews 13:4; 1 Thessalonians 4:3-8). In fact, we devote an entire session of the course to this topic.

Why do you think God would design sex to be enjoyed only within the context of marriage? Do you see any benefits to waiting?

_____

_____

_____

2.   Because the Scriptures are our authority and blueprint, because we care about you and because of the normal sexual pressures you face, we will ask you at different times in the weeks ahead how you are doing in this area. We sincerely want to see you build a strong foundation from the start in your marriage. How do you feel about this?

_____

_____

_____

3. Can you tell me what your physical involvement with each other has been up to this point?

_____

_____

_____

_____

What are your boundaries?

_____

_____

_____

_____

4. Are you willing to abstain from sexual involvement until your marriage?

_____

_____

_____

_____

overview of PREPARING for marriage

> **Note:** The information on these pages is not to be given to the premarried couple, but explain it either by reading or telling them.

Goals

We desire that each participant:

- Be exposed to the important building blocks for a healthy Christian marriage;
- Know what a Christian marriage looks like;
- Develop the skills to lay a good foundation from the beginning;
- Know how to evaluate whether God would have you marry each other, and whether this is the right time to marry.

Significance

We consider this a vital study that will help you lay a solid foundation for marriage. You must be willing to make this a very high priority for each session. If you really love this person that you are considering marrying, the time you put into this study will demonstrate how much you care and how much you want what God desires in a marriage.

Format

Preparing for Marriage includes two primary components:

MAIN SESSIONS

In each of the six main sessions couples will learn more about how to make a marriage work, then interact with each other to apply the material to their relationship. These sessions are contained in parts two and three of the workbook.

Here's what you will find in each session:

> **True North**—A statement of the biblical truth related to the topic you are covering
>
> **Get the Picture**—An introduction to the topic that gives them the opportunity to answer questions and complete exercises that allow them to grasp the topic and understand why it is important
>
> **Get the Truth**—The Bible discovery section of each chapter in which they examine and discuss biblical truths to learn God's principles on different aspects of marriage
>
> **Navigating by True North: Truths to Chart Your Course**—Summary statements of the key principles from each session
>
> **Couple's Project**—The interaction portion of the session includes the following sections:
>
> > **Get Real**: Questions to guide discussion
> >
> > **Get to the Heart of Your Marriage—Prayer**: An opportunity to pray together and experience a spiritual discipline that will be one of the keys to their growing marriage in the years to come
> >
> > **Get Deeper**: Optional assignments for the highly motivated—those who want to go where no engaged couple has gone before!
> >
> > **Questions for Those Who Were Previously Married**

In addition, several of the sessions include bonus projects designed to help couples deepen their experience as they work through the course.

SPECIAL PROJECTS

These are five projects that will guide couples in discussions of critical issues and help them learn even more about one another. These projects include:

- The "Personal History Worksheet" has dozens of questions designed to help them understand their past and share it with one another.

- The "Great Expectations" helps a couple understand the expectations they are bringing into their marriage.
- "Evaluating Your Relationship" provides a framework to ask some challenging questions about their relationship.
- "A Decision-Making Guide" is designed to help them discern God's will for their relationship.
- The "Purity Covenant" provides an opportunity to commit themselves to sexual purity before they are married.

About the Mentoring Couples

The words in the parentheses are for those who are conducting this interview but are not the mentoring couple.

1. We are (The mentor couple is) willing to let you observe our (their) marriage, ask questions and listen to our (their) failures and successes.

2. All mentor couples have been trained and screened by the church.

3. You will meet with us (them) _____ times privately. (If you are using the small-group format, also tell them how many group sessions there will be.)

4. We (They) want to be good resources and friends for you in the future.

Other Information

CHURCH POLICY ON WEDDINGS

YOUR FIRST COUNSELING SESSION

Date:_____

Place:_____

Time:_____

FAMILYLIFE MARRIAGE CONFERENCE

We encourage you to attend a FamilyLife Marriage Conference. This conference will only add to your growth during this critical decision-making time about marriage.

INterview summary

To be completed after the meeting

1. What were your overall impressions of this couple?

2. What level of emotional maturity does the couple bring to this relationship?

3. What level of spiritual maturity do you see in each person?

4. What strengths do they exhibit that will help their relationship?

5. What concerns/red flags need to be explored and addressed further?

6. Were they informed on church wedding policies?

❑ yes   ❑ no

7. Did you share the gospel with them?

❑ yes   ❑ no

Results:

_____

_____

_____

_____

8. Other comments:

_____

_____

_____

_____

PeRSONaL WORKBOOK Notes

Following are comments and suggestions for all of the sessions and special couple's projects, in the order they appear in the personal workbook.

For every session and project we include general comments and for most we include suggestions of things for you to share with the couple as their mentor.

As we stated in the previous section, there are several options for guiding a couple through this study:

- If you are leading a couple through the workbook your-self, it is assumed that you will ask all of the questions in order as you go through the "Get the Picture and "Get the Truth" sections in each session.
- If you are meeting with the couple after they have already completed each session and project on their own,

suggested discussion questions for each session are included in this chapter.

- If you are meeting with the couple individually after they've already met in a small group to go through the material, discussion questions for each session are also included.
- Finally, if you are counseling a couple and one or both people were married previously, be sure to ask them how they answered the extra questions at the end of each session's couple's project.

special project 1

personal history worksheet

General Comments

1. Although premarried couples know a lot about each other, this worksheet will help them learn a lot more! It will also help alert all of you to any potential problems arising from the past. Most premarried couples don't realize what they don't know about marriage. In other words, they have no clue how problems from the past will affect their marriage.

    For example, an increasing number of young people marrying today grew up in homes torn apart by divorce or other dysfunctions. They observed a failed marriage and many may have never observed a marriage that worked properly. Unless they take an honest look at the past and determine how it has affected them, they may be unable to prevent themselves from walking down the same path.

2. Some Christians may deny the influence of the past, citing 2 Corinthians 5:17, which tells us that we are "new creatures in Christ." It's true that we have been forgiven, but our new life in Christ does not mean that the scars of the past have disappeared. There are consequences to the choices we make, both good and bad. There are also consequences to the choices our parents made.

3. We suggest that couples fill out the worksheet individually, then meet together to share their answers. At some point during your personal meetings with them, you should discuss the project with them. You probably don't have time to go through the entire worksheet with them, so here is a suggested sequence for your discussion:

    a. Ask, "What did you think of the Personal History Worksheet?"

b. Ask, "What were some of the most interesting or important things you've learned about each other?"

c. In "Section One: Your Relationship History," ask how they answered questions 2 and 4.

d. In "Section Two: Your Family," ask how they answered the questions under "Home Environment" and "Parents."

e. In "Section Three: Your Spiritual Journey," ask how they answered questions 1 and 4.

Be on the alert for any major issues that may come up during your discussion. If the woman mentions, for example, that her father deserted the family when she was a young girl, you will want to discuss this situation more thoroughly, either now or in the future.

4. *Sharing as a mentor:* Take a few minutes to read through the Personal History Worksheet and find some examples to share of issues about your past that you wish you had discussed before you were married. Perhaps you and your spouse came from very different family environments—socially, economically, relationally, etc. Talk about what you didn't know before you were married and how learning about your backgrounds helped you (or would have helped you) in specific ways.

5. If you have the opportunity to talk individually with each person, ask if it was hard for him or her to talk about the past, and why. Ask if there was anything about the past that he or she was reluctant to share.

6. Couples will discuss "Section Four: Your Life Map" in the Couple's Project at the end of Session Three.

special project 2

Great expectations

General Comments:

1. Each of us brings expectations into a relationship. Many of our expectations are neither good nor bad, but trouble develops when they conflict with those of our mates. Unresolved expectations often lead to demands, and demands lead to manipulation and conflict.

   Most premarried couples have thought very little about expectations. In fact, many couples spend years uncovering the expectations they bring into a marriage. This special project has two purposes: to uncover some of those expectations and to alert couples to the need to discuss their expectations.

2. Expectations come primarily out of our past experiences, so it is critical that you try to understand their family backgrounds and if they might be having a hard time coming up with some expectations, you can probably find them just from their background differences.

3. This project can be completed at any time, but we recommend that couples complete it before beginning the regular sessions of the workbook.

4. The first part of the project is an overview about expectations and a discussion about "Illusion and Reality." Here couples are confronted with a few common expectations that can seriously damage a relationship. Marriage is a wonderful institution, yet those who enter into it are, after all, only human. Couples need to understand that:

   - The intense feelings of love and passion they experience now will fade some after marriage—but those feelings can often be rekindled if we make romance a priority.
   - Life will not always be as exciting after marriage as it is when they are engaged.
   - Marriage is not always a cure for loneliness.

- Even though God brings two people together who will complete each other, they will not meet all of each other's needs. There are other needs that only other people can fill and some that only God can fill.
- They should not get married with the idea of making their mate a better person. This can happen, but it just as often does not.
- Marrying a Christian is not the *final* step to building a oneness marriage, it is only the beginning. That's why marrying someone *who is consistently and humbly walking before God* should be the more important criteria.

5. As with the Personal History Worksheet, you will want to discuss this subject of expectations at some time with the couple you are counseling. You will want to discuss the topic generally, then highlight a few areas they will need to discuss to avoid conflict soon into their marriage.

   Here is a suggested sequence:

   a. Ask, "Have you ever discussed this subject of expectations?"

   b. Ask how they answered the questions under the heading "Illusion and Reality."

   c. Ask if they discussed their expectations survey together, and whether they were able to apply the suggestions listed under "A Guiding Principle" and "Discussing Expectations."

   d. In the Expectations Survey, ask how they answered the following questions:
      - Question 1 under "Marriage Relationship"
      - Questions 1 through 7 under "Finances" (Another option is to save these questions for when you meet with them after Session Five on finances.)
      - Questions 3 and 4 under "Home"
      - Questions 1 through 4 under "Housekeeping"
      - Questions 1 and 2 under "Children and Parenting"
      - Questions 1 and 2 under "Spiritual Life"
      - Question 1 under "Holidays/Vacations/Special Occasions"
      - Question 5 under "Parents and Other Relatives"

♥   Questions 1 and 2 under "Sex" (Another option would be to save these questions for when you meet with them after Session Six on intimacy.)

6.   *Sharing as a mentor:* As you did with the Personal History Worksheet, look through the questions and think of some specific expectations you brought into marriage that were not discussed before the wedding. For example, you may have begun your marriage with the expectation that you would spend Christmas with your parents every year, then you discovered that your mate expected to spend the holidays with his or her parents. Talk about how you resolved—or didn't resolve—that difference.

SESSION ONE

WHY MARRIAGE?

General Comments

1. Most couples today have little idea what the Bible says about building a marriage and family. This session and the following one present God's blueprints for marriage through an intense examination of Genesis 1 and 2. By the end of Session One, couples should see that marriage is a much more important institution than they may have dreamed—at its core is a spiritual relationship between a man, a woman and the Lord God. Session Two then builds upon this idea by presenting God's plan for oneness.

2. At the same time, the two sessions lead the couples steadily to the realization that, in order to build a solid marriage, they need to take their marriage vows seriously. They need to receive each other as God's provision and make a lifelong commitment to oneness. If they are unable to make such a commitment to each other, they should cancel or postpone their wedding plans.

3. "Get the Picture" begins with the story of Bob and Sherry and their road to a oneness marriage. Case studies like this allow couples the freedom to discuss and learn from a hypothetical situation and not feel threatened even though the fictional relationship may, in fact, be very similar to their own.

   This story highlights how Bob and Sherry met and decided to marry. The story is typical in many ways because so many couples begin marriage with little idea of how to make it work.

4. "Get the Truth" discusses three purposes for marriage as outlined in the book of Genesis:

   a. *To mutually complete one another:* Many premarried couples will be able to grasp this concept because they're aware of many of their differences and they probably see those differences in a positive light. After marriage they may look at things differently, and it's sometimes a revelation for couples who have been married five or more years to think

of how they really do complete each other in a more profound way than they had ever realized.

b.   *To multiply a godly legacy*: While most couples want to start
a family, a significant number marry with no intention of
having children. Some say they want to focus on building
their careers while others believe they would not make
good parents. These couples need to be challenged with
the fact that the Bible does not make childbearing an
option. Some couples are unable to have children, but
those who can need to take some time to weigh their
desires in light of God's Word.

Most couples who do want children have given little
thought to the critical importance of parenting in God's
plan. This session could lead to some discussions about
when they want to begin a family and about their philoso-
phies of parenting.

c.   *To mirror God's image*: This is often the most difficult for
couples to understand. The final paragraph just before
question 10 is the critical one: "When people look at your
marriage, what will they see? Two people using each other
to meet their own needs and experiencing nothing but
conflict because of their selfishness? Or two imperfect people determined to love each other unconditionally and
reaching out to others with the overflow of that love? In a
time when about 50 percent of marriages eventually end
in divorce, a successful marriage becomes a testimony of
God's love and power."

5.   Since this is the first session and much of this information may
be new to a couple, don't press too hard about how they are
going to apply these principles in their relationship. You'll have
the opportunity to give them a stronger challenge during the
next session.

6.   Encourage the couple to complete the Parental Wisdom Project
at the end of the Couple's Project. It will help them learn more
about marriage, and it will also give them the chance to connect with their parents.

7.   *Sharing as a mentor*: When discussing how God brings together
a man and woman to complete one another, tell the couple
some of the different ways you and your mate fill each other's

gaps. Tell them some of the things you continue to learn about this even after years of marriage.

If you have children, during the section on leaving a godly legacy talk about some of your goals as a parent. Tell them about what you've done to help your children grow up to know and love the Lord.

The section on mirroring God's image will become clearer to the couples if you are able to give them an example of how you have seen part of God's character revealed in the marriage of your own parents or of someone you know.

If you are meeting with the couple after they have completed the session on their own:

a. Ask, "What were some things that you learned about God's purposes for marriage as you completed this session?"

b. Ask, "What did you learn about yourself during this session?"

c. Ask, "What did you learn about your fiancé(e) during this session?"

d. In "Get the Picture," ask how they answered question 2.

e. In "Get the Truth," ask how they answered questions 1, 5 through 9.

f. In the Couple's Project, ask how they answered questions 2 and 3. Also, if someone has been previously married, discuss all the questions in "Questions for Those Who Were Previously Married."

If you are meeting personally with a couple after they already have participated in your small group:

a. Ask, "What were some things that you learned about God's purposes for marriage as you completed this session?"

b. Ask, "What did you learn about yourself during this session?"

c. Ask, "What did you learn about your fiancé(e) during this session?"

d. In "Get the Truth," ask how they answered questions 1, 5 through 9.

e.   In the Couple's Project, ask how they answered questions 2 and 3. Also, if someone has been previously married, discuss all the questions in "Questions for Those Who Were Previously Married."

SESSION TWO

GOD'S EQUATION FOR MARRIAGE: WHEN ONE PLUS ONE EQUALS ONE

General Comments

1. This session builds upon the truths presented in Session One. Continuing the Genesis story, it presents God's plan for marriage. The end of the session presents a summary of God's blueprints for marriage and confronts couples with two key questions they should be able to answer in the positive before moving toward marriage.

2. In "Get the Picture," the story of Bob and Sherry continues with some troubles they experience after they are married. These struggles highlight the problem of compatibility that undermines many marriages. This leads directly to the themes discussed in the remainder of the session.

3. "Get the Truth" then presents four parts of God's plan for marriage, four key commitments that are vital for premarried couples to make in order to build a oneness marriage:

    ♥ *Commitment Number One: Receive Your Mate*—This requires the ability to see that if God has given you a mate, this person is His provision for your needs. In the previous session the couples examined their respective strengths and weaknesses and determined how they complemented one another. They need to understand that they cannot enter marriage with the idea of changing the other person to meet their idealized version of a mate.

    ♥ *Commitment Number Two: Leave Your Parents*—The concept of leaving one's parents is important because when you marry, your relationship with your mate becomes a higher priority. Leaving one's parents doesn't mean abandoning them or breaking off the relationship. It just means that the marriage relationship has a higher priority that will sometimes lead to some difficult choices.

There are many ways newly married couples fail to leave their parents. They fail to leave *financially* by remaining dependent upon their parents for money. They fail to leave *emotionally* by remaining more attached to them than to their mates. In some cases, they fail to leave *physically* by living so close to them and seeing them so often that they undermine their new priority of making their marriage relationship work.

Leaving one's parents is especially difficult when the parents won't let go. Before a child is married, the wise parent will think through this issue and meet with the child to discuss how their relationship will change.

♥ *Commitment Number Three: Cleave to Your Mate*—Many couples today begin marriage with the idea that if it doesn't work, they can always get a divorce and try again. In fact, some marriage "experts" even claim that this process is healthy because couples can learn from their mistakes and build a better marriage the second time around.

The Scriptures make it clear, however, that God hates divorce. When two people are married, they make a sacred vow, a covenant between them and the Lord and He takes that covenant seriously.

By establishing the marriage relationship as a covenant, God sets it apart from every other relationship. From this new union a new family is formed. He designed marriage as a monogamous relationship with the opposite sex because He knew that for this relationship to work both people needed to be able to totally trust each other. And you can't trust another person who may bail out when the relationship becomes difficult.

♥ *Commitment Number Four: Become One Flesh*—Many singles believe that sex is merely a way of expressing love and getting to know one another, but God designed sexual intimacy with much more in mind. It is the final point in the bonding process. It is designed to follow commitment in marriage, not to precede it.

4. "Get the Truth" ends with a key section titled "A Oneness Marriage." Everything in Sessions One and Two lead to these few paragraphs, summarizing God's blueprints for marriage and challenging the couple to answer two key questions before they move toward marriage: "Is Christ at the center of your life?" and "Is God calling you together as man and wife?"

Since marriage is, at its heart, an intensely spiritual relationship between a man, a woman and God, you need to be comfortable with how the couple answers these questions before you counsel them to marry. If Christ is not at the center of both their lives, they will not be able to build their home on a solid spiritual foundation. If they do not have a conviction that God is leading them together, they will be unable to commit their lives to each other with the faith that God will make it possible for them to live up to that commitment.

These questions, in turn, lead the couple directly into the two Special Projects that follow: "Evaluating Your Relationship" and the "Decision-Making Guide." In these two projects, couples will take an in-depth look at their spiritual and relational compatibility and learn how to determine God's will concerning their decision to marry.

5. *Sharing as a mentor:* For each of the four commitments, try to think of something you can share from your own marriage. For "receive your mate," you could tell them about a time when you had to make a conscious decision after you were married to not regard your mate as an enemy but as God's provision for your needs.

For "leave your parents," you could talk about good and bad choices you've made in this area. This is one area where an unbiased adult can really help a young couple establish a healthy perspective. For example, you could talk to them about how to deal with the guilt a well-meaning parent may unfairly place upon them to come for visits or holidays.

For "cleave to your mate," you could tell about any temptations you've had to give up on your marriage or about friends and family who got divorced because they were unable to meet their commitments.

How you discuss "become one flesh" will depend on what you discussed about this area during the opening interview (see pages 37-56).

If you are meeting with the couple after they have completed the session on their own:

a. Ask, "What were some things that you learned about God's purposes for marriage as you completed this session?"

b. Ask, "What did you learn about yourself during this session?"

c. Ask, "What did you learn about your fiancé(e) during this session?"

d. For "Get the Picture," ask how they answered questions 1 and 2.

e. For "Get the Truth," ask how they answered questions 3 through 11.

f. Ask them how they would answer each of the two questions on pages 102-103 of the workbook at this point in their relationship:

♥ "Is Christ at the center of your life?" If the answer is no, you may need to explain the plan of salvation or talk to them about how to build a more solid relationship with God.

♥ "Is God calling you together as man and wife?" If they do not know how to answer this question, or if their answer seems vague, direct them to the two Special Projects that follow this session: "Evaluating Your Relationship" and "A Decision-Making Guide."

If you are meeting personally with a couple after they already have participated in the small group:

a. Ask, "What were some things that you learned about God's plan for marriage as you completed this session?"

b. Ask, "What did you learn about yourself during this session?"

c. Ask, "What did you learn about your fiancé(e) during this session?"

d. In "Get the Truth," ask how they answered questions 3 through 5 and 8 through 10.

e. Ask them how they would answer each of the two questions on pages 102-103 of the workbook at this point in their relationship:

- ♥ "Is Christ at the center of your life?" If the answer is no, you may need to explain the plan of salvation or talk to them about how to build a more solid relationship with God.
- ♥ "Is God calling you together as man and wife?" If they do not know how to answer this question, or if their answer seems vague, direct them to the two Special Projects that follow this session: "Evaluating Your Relationship" and "A Decision-Making Guide."

special project 3

evaluating your relationship

General Comments:

1. This special project is designed for each person to complete and then discuss together and with you. It goes hand-in-hand with "Special Project 2: A Decision-Making Guide."

2. Sessions One and Two lead a couple logically into these projects by slowly building up to the awareness that marriage is an intensely spiritual relationship between a man, a woman and their Lord. In order to build a oneness marriage, a couple must have Christ at the center of their lives, and they must know that God is calling them together as man and wife. So we strongly suggest completing this project and Special Project 4 after they've finished those sessions. However, these projects could be completed sometime later as long as they are finished before the workbook is completed.

3. Many premarried couples are so caught up in their emotions—either from the exhilaration of being in love or from the fear of commitment—that they are unable to think clearly about their relationship. This project is designed to help them do so by confronting their compatibility on two different levels—spiritual and relational.

4. Many couples face problems in marriage because they never asked each other difficult questions about spiritual compatibility. Many will adopt a pseudo-spirituality in order to win over the person they love. For example, a young man may become interested in a woman and quickly notice that God is an important part of her life. He may not have a relationship with God, but he starts going to church with her and shows interest in spiritual things. He learns how to sound spiritual, so he fools her into thinking he knows Christ. After the marriage, however, chances are that he will lose his interest and leave her feeling alone and betrayed.

5.   You could lead a couple or small group through the material in these first two special projects if you wish, but we suggest assigning the couples to complete them on their own and then meet with you. The real power of these projects will come as a couple spends time thinking and evaluating.

SPIRITUAL COMPATIBILITY

1.   As the workbook states, there are two key questions couples need to ask:

     ♥   Are both of you Christians?
     ♥   Do you both share the same commitment to spiritual growth and to serving God?

The first question is critical because 2 Corinthians 6:14,15 warns against Christians entering into *any* partnerships with unbelievers as it will be a relationship built on opposing values and goals. Building relationships on Christian values, trust and love is essential to the Christian life especially in the most intimate of all human relationships—marriage. When a believer marries an unbeliever, the relationship begins with incompatibility in the most important area of life because spirituality is the foundation on which every aspect of a person's life—goals, expectations and values—is built.

The second question addresses another important aspect of spiritual compatibility because there is a danger in one Christian marrying another who is much less mature and committed in the faith. This will probably lead to one of two things: Either the committed Christian will fall to the level of the other or the committed Christian will develop a growing frustration because his or her lifetime partner is unwilling to grow stronger in faith.

2.   If you completed the opening interview with the couple, you probably learned something of their spiritual backgrounds and were able to discern whether they were both Christians. If there is a problem in their spiritual compatibility and it was not confronted at that time, now is your opportunity as you meet with the couple and ask them how they answered questions 1 and 2.

3.   If you realize that both people are not Christians, this is a great

opportunity to explain the gospel. A copy of *The Four Spiritual Laws* by Bill Bright of Campus Crusade for Christ is included at the end of the workbook. We also urge you to exhort the couple to put the relationship on hold until they first establish a relationship with God. If God eventually calls them together, their marriage will only be stronger if they've learned how to walk with Him.

4. If you find that one person is a believer but the other is not, exhort the couple to either end the relationship or put it on hold. They should certainly put off any wedding plans. The Christian may believe he or she may win the other to Christ, but this is a dangerous goal because the nonbeliever may just put on a false front of repentance.

5. If both are Christians but one is apparently more committed to serving God, exhort them to postpone marriage plans so they can take more time to see if the relationship will work. They might even want to stop seeing each other for awhile.

RELATIONAL COMPATIBILITY

1. In the first part of this section we provide a very basic chart for evaluating how a couple's personalities and temperaments mesh. This chart, however, is really included just for those couples who are completing the study on their own, apart from a pastor, counselor or mentor. There are much better tools available for you to use, and we strongly recommend that you use one of the following:

You can order...

DiSC inventory for understanding behavior styles from: *Understanding One Another: A Personalized Guide to Better Communication,* Team Resources, Inc., 1994. It may be ordered from FamilyLife at 1-800-FL-TODAY.

Taylor-Johnson Temperament Analysis
Robert M. Taylor and Lucile Philips Morrison
Psychological Publications, Inc.,
5300 Hollywood Blvd.,
Los Angeles, CA 90027

PREPARE test
PREPARE Inc.
P. O. Box 190
Minneapolis, MN 55440

Myers-Briggs Type Indicator®
Consulting Psychologists Press
3803 East Bayshore Road
Palo Alto, CA 94303
800-624-1765

2.   The second part of this section is a list of relational "fog producers"—things that commonly cloud the thinking of someone
considering marriage. If you are meeting with a couple after
they've completed this project on their own, ask them which of
those fog producers they think apply to their relationship.

Be aware that the factors that cloud the thinking of many
premarried couples will also prevent them from recognizing
whether or not any of these fog producers are present. This is
your opportunity to talk to them about any fog producers that
you have noticed!

3.   The final part of this section is a list of relational "red flags."
These are serious relational problems that if present in a relationship, will cause serious problems unless they are confronted
and resolved before the wedding. In fact, some of these problems
may lead you to strongly recommend ending the relationship.

When meeting with the couple, ask if they think any of
these red flags apply to their relationship and be prepared to discuss any that they bring up. If you sense a reluctance on the part
of either person to answer this question, approach this person
privately and ask again—it could be that he or she is fearful of
bringing up the subject in the presence of the fiancé(e).

4.   Some couples are so caught up in their emotions and are moving so swiftly toward marriage that they fail to ask some tough
questions about whether this relationship is really heading in
the right direction. Others may have some doubts, but they fear
the embarrassment of halting wedding plans at a late date. If
you sense this is happening with the couple you are counseling,
you will need to give them two strong challenges:

First, *challenge them to seek guidance from God's Word and from trusted counselors*. Just as fog obscures reality by preventing us from spotting familiar buildings and landmarks, their emotions may prevent them from seeing the truth about their relationship.

Read Psalm 119:105,130: "Thy word is a lamp to my feet, and a light to my path. The unfolding of Thy words gives light; it gives understanding to the simple." Like an instruction book on how to operate your VCR, Scripture is a Christian's instruction book for life. You must not make a biblical decision apart from time spent in His Word studying His instructions.

Proverbs 11:14 points to another source of guidance—trusted counselors: "Where there is no guidance, the people fall, but in abundance of counselors there is victory."

What are their friends and family saying? If most of them are not positive about this relationship, they would be wise to learn why. If one or two people don't like this match, you could attribute their objections to personality differences or selfishness. But if quite a few family and friends disapprove, it could be that their emotions are blinding them.

Second, *challenge them to take the time they need to make a wise decision*. Ask if they think they've dated long enough to make a sound decision. Ask what they think would be the pros and cons of waiting another 6 to 12 months for the wedding.

If they are right for one another, their relationship *will* stand the test of time. They are, after all, about to commit themselves to loving and serving each other for a lifetime. It only makes sense to take the time they need to know whether they can truly make that commitment.

special project 4

a Decision-making guide: Helping you move from "do i?" to "i do!" or "i don't"

General Comments

1. This project guides couples in making the decision about whether or not they should marry. It helps them answer the question, "Is God leading us to be man and wife?" While we encourage them to complete it shortly after completing the special project on "Evaluating Your Relationship," couples should feel no pressure to make this decision yet. If you are counseling a couple that is struggling to determine God's direction, encourage them to read through this section and keep the concepts in mind as they complete the remainder of the workbook.

2. As with the previous project, you could lead a couple or small group through the material if you wish, but we suggest assigning the couples to complete it on their own and then meet with you.

3. Many Christians have an incomplete understanding of how to discern God's will. Some seek God's direction on minute daily decisions and look to discern God's supernatural leading in every circumstance of their lives. Others focus on the Bible and say that rather than trying to learn God's will we should be concerned about obeying God's will for our lives as revealed in Scripture and then using the sound mind God gives us to make the more difficult decisions.

   This Decision-Making Guide is built upon two principles. First, we believe the Bible contains most of what we need to know about God's will for our daily lives. Second, He also has given us the Holy Spirit who indwells, leads and guides us. The Holy Spirit will speak to us through God's Word, through prayer, through godly counselors and through desires and circumstances, building within us a conviction of what God is leading us to do in certain situations.

4. The first part of this project explains the components of a biblical decision. When meeting with the couple, ask if they feel they understood the section. Then turn to the heading, "How Does Your Wheel Look?" Ask how they answered the questions there.

5. The second part guides couples through a decision-making process. Walk through the five steps of this process with them. Ask:

    ♥ Did each of you spend time alone with God? How much?
    ♥ Did you declare your willingness to follow God's will? Why do you think this is important?
    ♥ Have you honestly evaluated your relationship?
    ♥ Do you think you are God's provision for each other? Why?
    ♥ When do you think is the right time to marry and why?

6. At a later time, you might want to confirm this decision with each person individually. This is especially important if you sense that one person is not being totally honest or realistic in the decision.

SESSION THREE

AUTHENTIC COMMUNICATION: AVOIDING THE POST-WEDDING LETDOWN

General Comments

1. Many couples experience such good communication during engagement they cannot comprehend the possibility that they would have difficulty after they are married. This is despite the fact that they've probably observed communication problems in the lives of other married couples—most notably their parents.

   This session is designed to give couples a few basics in communication and conflict resolution to help them avoid the "post-wedding letdown."

2. One major trend in our culture is an increasing difficulty in resolving conflict. Unresolved conflict leads to bitterness, isolation, and physical and emotional abuse. At its worst, it leads to assault and death. In this session couples will discuss their own history of resolving conflict and examine how they've worked out conflicts up to this point. They'll also learn about the importance of forgiveness.

3. Be sure to encourage the couple to complete the bonus "Couple's Interview Project" at the end of this session. This could be one of the most enjoyable projects they complete in the entire workbook. They could complete it with you and your mate or with another couple.

4. In "Get the Picture," the story of Bob and Sherry alerts couples to how easily communication problems can develop soon after they are married.

5. "Get the Truth" presents three lessons about communication:
   - Listening in order to understand;
   - Expressing oneself in order to be understood;
   - Resolving conflict.

Most of the material is pretty straightforward. For some couples it may not be new teaching. The question is how well they are applying it in their lives and in their relationship.

6. *Sharing as a mentor:* This is a great opportunity for you to take the biblical lessons of this session and bring them to life. Look through the three main topics—listening to understand, expressing to be understood and resolving conflict—think back through your marriage to find examples of failures and successes in each area. Tell them about conversations in which you did not listen to your mate and when you did. Think of conflicts that you resolved well and others that you did not. Tell about the consequences you've faced personally when you have not resolved conflict well.

Also, tell them that many of the problems they will eventually face as a couple will come not from a lack of skill in listening or expressing or resolving conflict. It will come from *not communicating at all!* That's why this study has so much interaction built into it—to help couples do so much communicating before marriage that they will continue to do so after the wedding.

If you are meeting with the couple after they have completed the session on their own:

a. Ask, "What were some things that you learned about communication and conflict as you completed this session?"

b. Ask, "What did you learn about yourself during this session?"

c. Ask, "What did you learn about your fiancé(e) during this session?"

d. Ask how they answered questions 1 and 2 after the Case Study in "Get the Picture."

e. Ask how they answered questions 1 through 4, and 7 through 9 in "Get the Truth."

f. Ask how they answered questions 3 through 8 in the Couple's Project. Also, if someone has been previously married, discuss all the questions in "Questions for Those Who Were Previously Married."

If you are meeting personally with a couple after they already have participated in your small group:

a.   Ask, "What were some things that you learned about communication and conflict as you completed this session?"

b.   Ask, "What did you learn about yourself during this session?"

c.   Ask, "What did you learn about your fiancé(e) during this session?"

d.   Ask how they answered questions 3 through 8 in the Couple's Project. Also, if someone has been previously married, discuss all the questions in "Questions for Those Who Were Previously Married."

session four

ROLes aND RespoNsibilities in marriage: movinG Beyond the cultural stereotype

General Comments

1. The purpose of this session is very simple—to provide couples with a biblical view of the roles of husband and wife in marriage. This will be a difficult subject for many couples to discuss because for the last few decades our culture has relentlessly attacked biblical roles and sexual identity. Most adults in America today are very confused about the differences between men and women and about how the different sexes should interact.

   As a mentor, it will be important for you to come to grips with what you believe the Bible says about roles for men and women in marriage. A resource we highly recommend is *Rocking the Roles*, by Robert Lewis and William Hendricks. This resource is available from FamilyLife by calling 1-800-FL-TODAY.

2. Be aware that this session is perhaps the longest in the workbook. If you are leading the session in a small group, you may wish to set aside some extra time to complete this session or divide it into two meetings.

3. In this session the couples are asked to think about how roles are portrayed in today's culture and how they have been influenced by these views. Be prepared to "prime the pump" for discussion by evaluating some of the current movies or television sitcoms and asking, "How does _____ portray roles in marriage?" or "How are husbands and wives portrayed on _____?"

4. "Get the Picture" leads the couples through Scriptures that describe core roles for the husband as the servant-leader and the wife as the helper-homemaker. It's important to keep

couples focused on what the Scripture says and challenge them to avoid interpreting the Bible with contemporary standards.

For example, when many people hear the word "leader" in the description of the core role for the husband, they often stereotype the leader in a marriage as a selfish tyrant who rules the house with an iron fist. The Bible, however, instructs husbands to love their wives "just as Christ also loved the church and gave Himself up for her" (Ephesians 5:25). This is quite a different picture of leadership than the one that our culture presents.

5. Many men have relinquished leadership of the home and have become passive. Indeed, this is the role many men marrying today will assume after they are married. A key challenge in this session is for men to accept responsibility and take the initiative in the home to be spiritual leaders.

6. *Sharing as a mentor:* Tell them about the roles and responsibilities you have assumed in your marriage and how you have learned to work as a team. If you have not always lived according to biblical roles, describe what roles you once assumed and how you have changed. Be honest about mistakes you've made and struggles you've faced.

If you are meeting with the couple after they have completed the session on their own:

a. Ask, "What were some things that you learned about roles as you completed this session?"

b. Ask, "What did you learn about yourself during this session?"

c. Ask, "What did you learn about your fiancé(e) during this session?"

d. In "Get the Picture," ask how they answered questions 2 and 3.

e. In the section on "God's Core Role for a Husband" in "Get the Truth," ask, "What do you think it means for a husband to love his wife as Christ loves the church?" Then ask how they filled out the chart in question 4. Finally, ask if they understand what submission means in Scripture.

f. In the section on "God's Core Role for a Wife" in "Get the Truth," ask, "What do you think it means for a wife to be a helper?" Then ask how they answered questions 7 through 11.

g. In the Couple's Project, ask how they answered questions 2 through 4. Also, if someone has been previously married, discuss all the questions in "Questions for Those Who Were Previously Married."

h. Ask if the couple completed the bonus project in which they wrote out a "Roles Position Statement." Encourage them to do so if they haven't. Explain that this will help them clarify what they understand about their roles and that they'll want to work on the project again after they are married.

If you are meeting personally with a couple after they already have participated in your small group:

a. Ask, "What were some things that you learned about roles as you completed this session?"

b. Ask, "What did you learn about yourself during this session?"

c. Ask, "What did you learn about your fiancé(e) during this session?"

d. For the section on "God's Core Role for a Husband" in "Get the Truth," ask, "What do you think it means for a husband to love his wife as Christ loves the church?" Then ask if they understand what submission means in Scripture.

e. For the section on "God's Core Role for a Wife" in "Get the Truth," ask, "What do you think it means for a wife to be a helper and a worker at home?" Then ask how they answered questions 9 and 10.

f. In the Couple's Project, ask how they answered questions 2 through 4. Also, if someone has been previously married, discuss all the questions in "Questions for Those Who Were Previously Married."

g. Ask if the couple completed the bonus project in which they wrote out a "Roles Position Statement." Encourage them to do so if they haven't. Explain that this will help them clarify what they understand about their roles. Suggest that they may want to also reevaluate their "Roles Position Statement" periodically after they are married.

session five

money, money, money

General Comments

1. The goals of this session are to provide premarried couples with a basic scriptural foundation for handling money and to guide them in discussing a few key issues that should be resolved before they are married.

   There are more than 2,000 verses in the Bible about finances and for good reason: how we handle our money is a good indicator of who we are and what we believe. God may use the area of finances as one way to test our faith, to see whether we are willing to trust Him.

2. Many couples fail to discuss this area in much detail before marriage. In fact, talking about finances may make them uncomfortable. It should not come as a surprise, then, that a high percentage of couples who divorce within five years of their wedding state that conflicts over finances were a major reason for their split.

   It is absolutely essential for couples to discuss their finances before marriage. If there is any problem in a relationship, chances are it will surface somehow in a financial decision. As financial counselor Larry Burkett says, "Money is the most common thing in our lives. If you're not communicating about money, you're not communicating about anything."

3. There are many reasons couples face such intense conflict about finances after they are married:

   ♥ Many people grow up with good training in many areas of life, but they have not been taught how to handle their finances. Many don't even know how to balance a checkbook.

   ♥ A growing number of young people are falling into debt, especially consumer debt with credit cards. Premarriage counselors report that they're seeing an increasing number of couples beginning marriage with a combined credit card debt of more than $10,000.

♥ God often brings opposites together in a marriage. A spender is often attracted to a saver, and vice versa. These differences quickly lead to conflict. (**Special note:** Contrary to the common stereotype, husbands generally cause more problems than wives with overspending. Financial counselors report that when women overspend, they do it on food and clothing. When husbands overspend, it's on big ticket items such as cars and boats.)

♥ Many couples make unwise financial decisions in their first year of marriage. They purchase a new car or a home, taking on large payments. Larry Burkett recommends that couples avoid purchasing a car or home during their first year of marriage.

♥ Because couples often don't want to talk about finances, they avoid discussing the very issues that could sabotage their relationship.

4. Because poor financial stewardship creates such a big problem in marriage, look closely for any signs of financial irresponsibility in those you counsel. One danger signal would be a large credit card debt. If you sense a big problem in this area, recommend to the couple that they postpone their marriage for 6-12 months to give them time to resolve their problems and clear up any debt.

   Chances are they will resist this idea, thinking that they surely could quickly solve any problems in this area after they are married. This attitude, however, only proves your point that they don't realize how big a problem they will have after they are married.

5. In "Get the Picture" you will find the final installment in the Bob and Sherry saga. This part of the case study presents in detail the different types of financial decisions that need to be made after a couple marries.

6. In "Get the Truth," couples are guided through Scriptures that establish two critical truths they need to understand about their finances:

   ♥ God owns everything.

♥ We are stewards of the money and resources that God has entrusted to us.

From that base, couples discuss some specific, practical areas of financial management in which to apply those biblical principles.

7. *Sharing as a mentor:* Tell the couple about how you have handled finances during your marriage. Tell them how you organize your finances and how you make decisions as a couple.

Be as honest as you can about what you've done well and what you've done poorly. Tell about some of your bad financial decisions—how and why you made them and the consequences you faced.

Also, challenge them about avoiding the materialism of our age. So many things we think we need are actually just desires influenced by advertising, by our emotions and our own selfishness. In order to follow God and not the world, we need to take a hard look at our materialistic attitudes.

If you are meeting with the couple after they have completed the session on their own:

a. Ask, "What were some things that you learned about finances as you completed this session?"

b. Ask, "What did you learn about yourself during this session?"

c. Ask, "What did you learn about your fiancé(e) during this session?"

d. In "Get the Picture," ask how they answered questions 1 through 3.

e. In "Get the Truth," ask how they answered questions 2, 5, 7, 10 and 11.

f. In the Couple's Project, ask how they answered questions 2 and 4. Also, if someone has been previously married, discuss all the questions in "Questions for Those Who Were Previously Married."

g. Ask if they completed the bonus project on setting a budget, and encourage them to do so if they have not.

If you are meeting personally with a couple after they already have participated in your small group:

a. Ask, "What were some things that you learned about finances as you completed this session?"

b. Ask, "What did you learn about yourself during this session?"

c. Ask, "What did you learn about your fiancé(e) during this session?"

d. In "Get the Picture," ask how they answered question 1.

e. In "Get the Truth," ask how they answered question 10.

f. In the Couple's Project, ask how they answered questions 2 and 4. Also, if someone has been previously married, discuss all the questions in "Questions for Those Who Were Previously Married."

g. Ask if they completed the bonus project on setting a budget, and encourage them to do so if they have not.

SESSION SIX

INTIMACY: SEXUAL COMMUNICATION IN MARRIAGE

General Comments

1. The goal of this session is to give couples a biblical view about sex. They'll learn about God's purposes for sex, and also about the differences between men and women in this area.

2. Many couples today almost have to be reprogrammed in this area. They have been so influenced by our culture that they are severely compromising God's standards about sexual purity. Hopefully you've already discussed this issue with the couple if you had them complete the Purity Covenant Project. If you did not, now would be the time to do so.

3. This may be a difficult session for you as the mentor because many of us are not accustomed to talking about sex with other people. Pray for wisdom about what to say, and for the ability to be transparent about this subject in an appropriate way.

4. We highly recommend that each couple obtain the book *Intended for Pleasure* by Ed and Gaye Wheat and read it together during the last month before marriage.

5. "Get the Picture" seeks to help couples think through where they have learned about sex. Many of us learn from the wrong sources and know little about what the Bible says. In fact, Christians are often stereotyped in the media as prudish, narrow zealots when it comes to this issue.

6. "Get the Truth" first presents the right perspective about sex: that it is God's idea and that it is much more than a mere physical act—it is a process of intimate communication. Then it discusses God's purposes for sex—procreation, pleasure, and protection from sin. Finally, a chart explaining the differences between men and women in the sexual area is presented.

7.   Be sure to mention the article at the end of the Couple's Project: "The Past: How Much Do I Share?" You don't need to read through it with them but explain that if they have questions about how much they should share, they might want to come and consult with you first.

8.   *Sharing as a mentor:* Without becoming too explicit, tell them about some of the mistakes you have made as a couple. The section in "Get the Truth" about differences between men and women should provide you with some good ideas. Tell them about the expectations you had about sex going into marriage and how those expectations influenced your attitudes and actions. Talk about things you have done to maintain romance and excitement in your marriage.

At some point you should talk to each person individually. If you are mentoring as a couple, you and your mate can talk with the person of the same sex. Ask more directly about what they anticipate in this area on the honeymoon and during the first year of marriage. Ask if they have any fears or questions.

If you are meeting with the couple after they have completed the session on their own:

a.   Ask, "What were some things that you learned as you completed this session?"

b.   Ask, "What did you learn about yourself during this session?"

c.   Ask, "What did you learn about your fiancé(e) during this session?"

d.   In "Get the Picture," ask how they answered questions 1 through 3.

e.   In "Get the Truth," ask how they answered questions 1, and 6 through 10.

f.   In the Couple's Project, ask how they answered questions 2 through 4. Also, if someone has been previously married, discuss all the questions in "Questions for Previously Married."

If you are meeting personally with a couple after they already have participated in your small group:

    a.   Ask, "What were some things that you learned as you completed this session?"

    b.   Ask, "What did you learn about yourself during this session?"

    c.   Ask, "What did you learn about your fiancé(e) during this session?"

    d.   In the Couple's Project, ask how they answered questions 2 through 4. Also, if someone has been previously married, discuss all the questions in "Questions for Previously Married."

a fiNaL pRoJect

This short project concludes the main sessions. It is designed for couples to complete on their own. Encourage them to complete it and then discuss it with you during your final session together.

This project first of all takes them back once more to their decision to marry. Is it a solid relationship built on the true foundation—Jesus Christ? Are they ready to commit to each other? If so, they are asked to sign a statement indicating their commitment to receive each other as God's provision. Then they are encouraged to select a Scripture verse that will be a foundation for their marriage and family.

special project 5

purity covenant

1. We suggest giving this project to couples before they complete the workbook, particularly during the third special project "Evaluating Your Relationship."

2. In a culture such as ours, it's increasingly difficult to stay morally pure before marriage. Many premarried Christian couples are also compromising in this area, but God's standards are clear— He wants us to be morally pure.

3. There are two purposes to this project. The first is to briefly define God's biblical standards for moral purity. The second is to challenge couples to sign a "Purity Covenant" in which they promise to remain pure until their honeymoon.

4. It will require a great deal of courage for you to confront couples in this area. You will need to ask them directly if they are staying morally pure, and you will need to exhort them to break off any physical relationship before marriage.

Premarital Couple evaluation

Fill out this evaluation at the end of the course.

Premarital Couple   **Mentoring Couple**

Male _____   Male _____

Female_____   Female_____

1.   Circle the sessions that the premarital couple attended.

    1   2   3   4   5   6

    Any comments:

_____

_____

_____

_____

2. Circle the sessions in which the couple completed their homework.

    1   2   3   4   5   6

3. Did you read the couple's "Personal History Worksheet?"

    ❑ Yes   ❑ No

4. Did the couple discuss the in-law questionnaire with their parents?

    ❑ Yes   ❑ No

5. Did the couple receive sufficient input concerning the personality testing instrument that was used?

    ❑ Yes   ❑ No

6. How many times did you meet with the couple outside the group? _____

7. Did the couple remain sexually pure during this time frame?

    ❑ Yes   ❑ No

    Did you ask them a couple of times about this and get their specific responses?

    ❑ Yes   ❑ No

8. Observations: Check the box if the answer is yes:

		M	F
a.	Do they communicate and listen well?	❑	❑
b.	Are they flexible?	❑	❑
c.	Are they teachable?	❑	❑
d.	Do they have a realistic picture of a Christian marriage?	❑	❑
e.	Do they have a reasonable understanding of each other's pasts?	❑	❑
f.	Do they have good conflict resolution skills?	❑	❑
g.	Is Christ a vital part of their lifestyle?	❑	❑

h. What other strengths does this couple exhibit?

_____

_____

_____

_____

i. Suggested areas of needed improvement?

_____

_____

_____

_____

9. How do you think this couple grew in their relationship from the beginning to the end of this course?

_____

_____

_____

_____

10. Would you recommend that this couple marry? Why?

_____

_____

_____

_____

If not, why not?

_____

_____

_____

_____

Or would you recommend they delay their marriage plans? Why? For how long?

_____

_____

_____

_____

11. After marriage, what future recommendations would you specifically offer for this couple to strengthen their relationship further?

_____

_____

_____

_____

about the authors

David Boehi is the editor of Real FamilyLife magazine and of the HomeBuilders Couple's Series®.

Jeff Schulte and **Lloyd Shadrach** are former FamilyLife staff members who are now pastors in Nashville, Tennessee.

Brent Nelson is also a former FamilyLife staff member who presently works as a salesman in Birmingham, Alabama.

about the general editor

Dennis Rainey is Executive Director of FamilyLife, host of "FamilyLife Today" radio show and the author of several best-selling books, including *Moments Together for Couples* (Regal Books, 1995).

Bless Your Home.

Marriage-building resources from Regal Books.

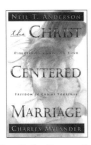

The Christ-Centered Marriage

Neil T. Anderson and Charles Mylander

This engaging book will show you and your spouse how to work together to securely set your marriage on a Christ-centered foundation and experience renewed intimacy, joy and fulfillment.

Paperback
ISBN 08307.18494

Spiritual Protection for Your Children

Neil T. Anderson and Pete & Sue Vander Hook

This is the incredible true story of a family that found themselves at the center of a satanic assault. This book will equip you to resist the enemy and protect your children by claiming your family's identity in Christ.

Paperback
ISBN 08307.18680

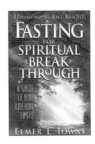

Fasting for Spiritual Breakthrough

Elmer Towns

This book explores the biblical foundations for fasting and introduces you to nine biblical fasts—each designed for a specific physical and spiritual outcome.

Paperback
ISBN 08307.18397

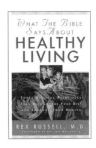

What the Bible Says About Healthy Living

Rex Russell, M.D.

The definitive diet plan taken straight from God's Word! These biblical principles for healthy eating and living will help you improve your physical—and spiritual—health.

Paperback
ISBN 08307.18583

Moments Together for Couples

Dennis and Barbara Rainey

This easy-to-use, best-selling 365-day devotional will give you and your spouse a chance to pause, relax and draw upon the strength of the Lord every day.

Hardcover
ISBN 08307.17544

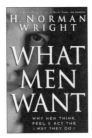

What Men Want

H. Norman Wright

Every man has questions. Here's a book with answers! For men, it's a clear look at God's plan for true manhood. For women, it's a revealing look at why men think and act the way they do.

Hardcover
ISBN 08307.15932

Starting Out Together Devotional

H. Norman Wright

A great beginning for dating or engaged couples, this dynamic 60-day devotional will help them to start their days and lives together focused on God.

Hardcover
ISBN 08307.18761

The Secrets of a Lasting Marriage

H. Norman Wright

Love can last for a lifetime. Here is a clear, practical plan to help couples reignite a love that is fading, or reinforce a love that is still going strong.

Hardcover
ISBN
08307.17498

Ask for these resources at your local Christian bookstore.

Regal
A Division of Gospel Light

Be a HomeBuilder in Your Community.

Y ou've just finished one of the most important construction projects in your life—helping couples grow closer to each other and to God. But the work doesn't stop when the foundation is laid. You can continue helping couples build a solid framework for their marriages by introducing them to **The HomeBuilders Couples Series®**. Hundreds of thousands of couples across the nation have already begun to build stronger marriages in **HomeBuilders** small groups. Even first-time group leaders can lead these studies at home, comfortably and with confidence. It's a fun way for couples to get closer to each other and to God—and a great way to get to know their neighbors.

Building Your Marriage
By Dennis Rainey
Help couples get closer together than they ever imagined possible.
•Leader's Guide
ISBN 08307.16130
•Study Guide
ISBN 08307.16122

Building Your Mate's Self-Esteem
By Dennis & Barbara Rainey
Marriage is God's workshop for self-esteem.
•Leader's Guide
ISBN 08307.16173
•Study Guide
ISBN 08307.16165

Building Teamwork in Your Marriage
By Robert Lewis
Help couples celebrate and enjoy their differences.
•Leader's Guide
ISBN 08307.16157
•Study Guide
ISBN 08307.16149

Resolving Conflict in Your Marriage
By Bob & Jan Horner
Turn conflict into love and understanding.
•Leader's Guide
ISBN 08307.16203
•Study Guide
ISBN 08307.16181

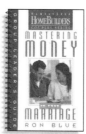

Mastering Money in Your Marriage
By Ron Blue
Put an end to conflicts and find out how to use money to glorify God.
•Leader's Guide
ISBN 08307.16254
•Study Guide
ISBN 08307.16246

Growing Together in Christ
By David Sunde
Discover how Christ is central to your marriage.
•Leader's Guide
ISBN 08307.16297
•Study Guide
ISBN 08307.16289

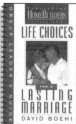

Life Choices for a Lasting Marriage
By David Boehi
Find out how to make the right choices in your marriage.
•Leader's Guide
ISBN 08307.16262
•Study Guide
ISBN 08307.16270

Managing Pressure in Your Marriage
By Dennis Rainey & Robert Lewis
Learn how obedience to God will take pressure off your marriage.
•Leader's Guide
ISBN 08307.16319
•Study Guide
ISBN 08307.16300

Expressing Love in Your Marriage
By Jerry & Sheryl Wunder and Dennis & Jill Eenigenburg
Discover God's plan for your love life by seeking God's best for your mate.
•Leader's Guide
ISBN 08307.16661
•Study Guide
ISBN 08307.16688

FAMILYLIFE   Look for **The HomeBuilders Couples Series®** at your local Christian bookstore.

Gospel Light